Contents

	Page
First movement	2
Next door's dinosaur	4
Down at the Dinosaur Fair	6
Dinosaur fun	10
Reptile	12
A mouse in the kitchen	14
Superhero	16
The puppeteer	20
Star night	22
A candle to the sun	24

Nelson

First movement

I'm training for the race,
so give me some space ...
stretch your arms in the air,
shake the cobwebs from your hair!

I'm training for the race,
so give me some space ...
an athlete never lingers,
so wiggle all your fingers!

I'm training for the race,
so give me some space ...
creak like the trees
when you're bending at the knees!

I'm training for the race,
so give me some space ...
breathe in, fill your lungs,
stick out wiggly wormy tongues!

I'm training for the race,
so give me some space ...
give it all you've got,
jogging on the spot!

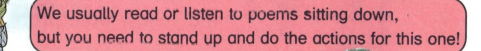

We usually read or listen to poems sitting down, but you need to stand up and do the actions for this one!

Next door's dinosaur

Do your neighbours have a puppy?
Do they keep a family cat?
Well, the folk who live next door to us
have a dinosaur called Drat!

It must have been a year ago
they heard thumping at the door,
and when they went to answer it
they were shocked by what they saw!

Standing squarely in the garden,
her neck stretched to the roof,
was Drat the dreaded dinosaur
in a yellow waterproof!

Drat quickly made herself at home
(for breakfast she liked kippers);
she stomped around in a dressing gown
and a pair of pure wool slippers!

She's tried sleeping on the sofa,
she's tried sleeping in the bed;
but every time she tossed and turned,
she bumped her bulky head.

Now her tail fits in the bedroom,
her back legs fill the bath;
her neck twists round the living room,
then up the garden path!

Dinosaurs became extinct 65 million years ago, long before humans appeared on Earth. Would you like to have had a dinosaur as a pet?

Down at the Dinosaur Fair

You can turn,
you can twist
in the prehistoric mist,
feel the dampness in your hair.
You can sprint,
you can spin
from a big bony chin,
down at the Dinosaur Fair!

You can swoop,
you can swing
from a dark leather wing,
and fly through pillows of air.
You can slip,
you can slide
on a scaly scarlet hide,
    down at the Dinosaur Fair!

You can zing,
you can zoom
down a backbone flume,
whizz round in a waltzing chair.
You can whip,
you can whack
on a slippy saddleback,
    down at the Dinosaur Fair!

I'm sure young dinosaurs were playful little creatures, much like kittens, lion cubs and baby chimps today.

You can trip,
you can trek
up a narrow bendy neck,
any day, any time, anywhere.
You can flail,
you can float
like a wave-tossed boat,
    down at the Dinosaur Fair!

Dinosaur fun

To keep the dinosaurs cool,
there's a fresh whirlpool
filled with bubbling waters.
It's a place to meet
for a special treat;
it's fun for sons and daughters!

On the hot red rocks
they take off their socks;
they stretch and bend at the knee.
They backflip in
with their multicoloured skin,
and float like ships on the sea.

All the long day
the dinosaurs play,
until the sun sets red in the west.
They splish and splash,
and bump and crash;
then they jog home to their nest!

Picture a hot desert, the sun beating down and the young dinosaurs doing their daily routine - keeping cool at the local leisure centre!

Reptile

Slip, slide, slither,
the snake will shake and shiver.

Slither, slip, slide,
dark is the dinosaur's hide.

Slide, slither, slip,
dragon's tail a swishing whip.

Slither, slip, slide,
see the tortoise slowly glide.

A mouse in the kitchen

There's a mouse in the kitchen,
playing skittles with the peas.
He's drinking mugs of coffee
and eating last week's cheese.

There's a mouse in the kitchen;
we could catch him in a hat.
Or else he'll toast the teacakes
and that will annoy the cat.

There's a mouse in the kitchen,
ignoring all our wishes.
He's eaten tomorrow's dinner ...
but at least he's washed the dishes.

Yes, I'm the mouse in the kitchen;
thank you for the grub.
I feel quite full but thirsty now,
so I'm nipping down the pub!

Superhero

When the President has been kidnapped
by crazed, evil crooks;
when the library sends you letters
saying pay for lost books;
just send for
Super-Spider-Bat-Hulk-Man!

If Earth is being threatened
by creatures from space;
if school sports are boring
and you don't win a race;
just give him a call:
Super-Spider-Bat-Hulk-Man!

When your school work's too hard
and your best mark is zero;
don't let it upset you;
just call our great hero:
Super-Spider-Bat-Hulk-Man!

So if danger's approaching
and the whole town is on fire;
if you rip your pants
on a piece of barbed wire;
who ya gonna call?
Super-Spider-Bat-Hulk-Man!

Forget Wonderwoman, Superman and Batman - Super-Spider-Bat-Hulk-Man can bend chips, tear up bus tickets and chase spiders down the bath plughole!

The puppeteer

On the top shelf the soldier,
the dragon, the doll;
the red-cheeked policeman,
his ear to the wall ...

A crestfallen teddy,
the robot and Punch
have long left the funfair
and gone off to lunch.

Next to the cowboy
sits Gingerbread Man.
His eyes do not sparkle;
he says, "Laugh if you can."

Rows of blank faces
with sad, empty eyes;
mouths without words,
without songs, without sighs.

The fireman is frowning,
the pierrot cries;
for puppets stop living
when their puppeteer dies.

I wrote this poem after hearing about the death of a man who performed puppet shows for children.
With no one to make them come alive, perhaps the puppets also died ... sor

Star night

It's the first clear night of winter,
a night as clear as polished glass.
My dad fetches the telescope from the attic
where it lives next to old books
and bags full of old clothes.

The telescope stands to attention
on its three spindly legs in the garden.
"Ooohhh!" says my dad, peering into it.
"Look!" he tells me.

I look but I can only see the roof.

A candle to the sun

The sun is like a searchlight;
it scorns, it scalds, it scorches;
the light of stars is dimmer,
a swarm of distant torches.

The planets shed their lamplight,
ashen grey or pepper red;
the moonglow, pale as snowdrops
scatters petals on my bed.

I have always written poems about the stars, the sun and the moon. This poem is about all the different kinds of light that the heavenly bodies beam down at us.